Timeless Lifetime Book of the Universe

I discovered
the
ANCIENT SECRETS
of the
FOUNTAIN OF YOUTH!

"The Golden Key to Unlock the Hidden
Door of the Profound Treasure Within"

ANGELIE BLISS

Published by Air & Water King, Inc.

520 Broadway
Truth or Consequences, New Mexico 87901
U.S.A.

Written in Molokai, Hawaii 96748 U.S.A.
Cover picture taken by Angelie Bliss
Author's picture taken by John S. Bliss

First published - U.S.A. & Philippines 1996

Distributed to the Whole World

FOREVER YOUNG Club®
Printed in the United States of America
Arrow Graphics, Inc., Watertown, MA 02172

Library of Congress Catalog Card Number: 96-84089
ISBN: 0-9651438-3-X

CONTENTS

FOREWORD

One **who understands** this book,
Will not tamper with what is written;
No words are to be omitted or added;
For this is an **open "Book of Understanding"**
To one who is searching the **true** meaning,
Of the **profound** secrets of living.

and

One **who doesn't understand** this book,
Will tamper with what is written;
Words will be omitted or added;
To **close** the **"Book of Understanding"**,
And the **false** meaning of "Fountain of Youth",
Will remain **surface** as it is, forever.

Angelie Bliss
Authoress

1

DEDICATION

This book is dedicated to my beloved family who sincerely supported my beliefs in life and also to those who are still skeptical; to my Spirit Master who guides and teaches me the **"Knowledge of Understanding"**; to my love ones who are on the other side; to my teachers; to my students; to Halau Hula 'o Kilohana; to the members of Forever Young Club and to you, dear reader.

* *

INTRODUCTION
Is the Fountain of Youth
a fact or fiction?

* *

Does the Fountain of Youth truly exist? What is it? Is it really for real? Well, you will be the only one to answer these questions. To me, the Fountain of Youth truly exists and I'll tell you why I firmly believe in this and what it means to me.

I'd like to share with you my experiences, discoveries, and knowledge of **"half part of our real world"** which is our **"unseen world"**. I will bring you step by step to a path of understanding and help you find your way to discover the true meaning of the Fountain of Youth.

It will be **easier** for you **to understand** this book if you will set aside for awhile your negative thoughts, negative feelings, the negative way you feel toward others, and your own religious beliefs while you're reading this. Just **keep the positive side** with you and **feel loved** and **open**. You are one of the chosen to really discover and understand the Fountain of Youth especially when you experience the priceless gift that GOD already gave you (as most people are not aware of it) and you will, as long as you have faith. Just nurture that faith with love and you'll see, you will have the confidence to answer positively to the questions above.

7

* *

LIFE IS FULL
OF
MYSTERIES

* *

When I was a child, I had experienced many amazing things that most people think is unbelievable, especially those who only believe the things that is scientifically proven. I was born and raised in the Philippines. To think about it, I feel lucky because even though I grew up without many material things, I was closer to spirituality. We have always been told true stories by my grandparents, parents, relatives and friends about the "unseen world". The **unseen world** nowadays are thought by most people to be superstitious and unbelievable.

Besides the stories I have heard, I have experienced myself these mysterious phenomena that frightened me as I had no knowledge to what was going on at that time. And it is true that **if we don't understand something, we are afraid of it** and most people want to close their mind and don't want to hear anymore about it. This causes them to bury their "**treasure**" deeper and as a result, making them harder to find. For some reason, even though I had experienced the frightening things, I was curious to learn more about it. I started reading books of the unknown mysteries, did research, studied it, practiced it, and with the guidance of my Spirit Master, I learned to understand it. Then I began to realize that it is not so fearful after all!

THE UNKNOWN MYSTERIES

We call it "Unknown Mystery": if it is not scientifically proven; if nobody can prove the things that our five senses can perceive; if it is not understood in one's religion; and if it is confusing for us to understand how it works and how it happens. A few names that deal with the unknown mysteries are:

*AKUA   *ANGELS   *AURA
*ALIENS   *CHI   *CLAIRAUDIENCE
*CLAIRVOYANCE   *DIYOS   *DREAM
*ESP(Extra Sensory Perception)
*ESPIRITU   *FAITH HEALING
*FAIRIES   *FENG SHUI
*FOUNTAIN OF YOUTH   *GOD
*GHOST   *KI
*MENTAL TELEPATHY   *PRANA
*REIKI   *QABALA
*REINCARNATION   *SPIRIT
*SHAMAN   *TAO   *TELEKINESIS
*UFO(UNIDENTIFIED FLYING OBJECT)
*UNIVERSE   *VOODOO   *YOGA

I could probably go on and on naming the unknown mysteries or you probably have names that you can add on the lists above in your own language. These are actually not mysteries at all if we really know how to understand each one of them, what they really mean, and how they work.

THE TRUTH IS, THEY ARE JUST WORDS OR NAMES!

THE KNOWN MYSTERIES

The "Known Mystery" is what we call something: if it is scientifically proven; if we can perceive things with our five senses; if we know who it is in the religion we are in; and if we think we understand how things work and happen. Here are a few names of our known mysteries:

*ART　　　*BIBLE　　*BIRTH　　*BOOK
*BUDDHA *CHRIST　*CONFUCIUS
*DANCE　*DEATH　*EARTH
*ELECTRICITY *ELECTRIC FIELD
*ENERGY　　*FACSIMILE MACHINE
*FIRE　*GRAVITY　　*HUMAN BEING
*IDENTIFIED FLYING OBJECT　*LAO TZU
*LIGHTNING　　*LOVE　　*MIND
*MEDICAL HEALING　　　*MOON
*MUSIC　　*POETRY *RADIO WAVE
*SEX　　　*SONG　　*STAR　　*SUN
*TELEPHONE *TELEVISION　*WATER

These are just a few names of the known mysteries and again you can add your own words to name the known mysteries. You might wonder why the names above are considered as mysteries. You will find it out along the lines.

If one sees it, they believe it;
If one hears it, they listen to it;
If one smells it, they inhale it;
If one tastes it, they swallow it;
If one touches it, they love it;
But if one doesn't understand it,
they are afraid of it!

THE KNOWN AND UNKNOWN MYSTERIES

These two kinds of mysteries are not different from each other if we know how to balance these opposites to **unite** into **one**.

It is easier for you to understand this, if your mind is open. I recommend for you **not to try too hard to analyze** this as this will only open the door to confusion and causes to close one's mind. **Just let it flow through your open mind** and you will begin to understand this profound knowledge. Be patient.

The "KNOWLEDGE OF UNDERSTANDING" can not enter inside a closed mind as a person can not enter inside the house if the door is closed.

* *

UNIVERSAL SYMBOL

* *

THE BALANCE OF ALL OPPOSITES

Few examples of the opposites are: good-bad; known-unknown; up-down; right-left; light-dark; open-close; full-empty; rise-sink; positive-negative; birth-death; heavy-light; love-hate; courage-fear; over-under; happy-sad; relax-tense; inhale-exhale; young-old; in-out; beginning-end; yin-yang; east-west; north-south; mental-physical; mind-body; etc.

☯ is a symbol of **UNITY**. Where the beginning meets the end. The symbol signifies that it only ends where it started. To become one, one should balance the opposites. When opposites are balanced, they become the "SINGLE DIVINE PRINCIPLE". This principle helps and guides me to keep my entire being balanced as a whole.

TO UNITE THE OPPOSITES,
THEY SHOULD BE BALANCED;
TO BALANCE THE OPPOSITES,
THERE SHOULD BE A CENTER;
AND

NOTHING

IS THE CENTER OF THE OPPOSITES.

BALANCING THE OPPOSITE

Too much is not balanced and too little is not balanced. Over is not balanced and under is not balanced. Greater is not balanced and less is not balanced.

Too much belief of the unknown is not balanced as one doesn't want to be a part of the known. And too much belief of the known is not balanced as one can not see the unknown. To balance the two, we have to open our awareness to both sides so we can see that the two are actually the other half of each other. To balance it, we will unite them into one.

* *

ESPIRITU

* *

The Chinese called it Chi or Qi; the Japanese called it Ki; in India they call it Prana; to others, they call it Spirit or Soul; in science, they call it Energy or Force. Whatever you call it, is your choice.

I call it in our Philippine language, **"Espiritu"** (pronounced as es-pee-ree-too). Espiritu is derived from Spanish word of spirit. This is our **"unseen world"**. Nobody sees it, but it is there. This is the one that keeps us alive in a physical form. Without Espiritu, we can not exist on earth in our human form.

It is true that the **human body, is one's life**. We put all our attention to our physical body and learned how to work with it. This full attention to human body causes us to forget the other half of its opposite, the **mind**.

Nobody can see one's mind but this is **the other half of one's life**, too.

Living
Is
Full
Espiritu

THE TIME WHEN I WAS NOTHING

I experienced "NOTHING" during my solemn meditation.

During my meditation, I went back to my childhood, then back to my mother's womb, then to **emptiness, peace, just nothing**... then back in 1947 in another physical form in a different place. When I came back out from my meditation, I wondered why I was back in 1947?...Wait a minute, I wasn't born in that year yet, I said to my outer self. Then my inner self said that it is true that my present form didn't exist during that time. My other physical form died in 1947, and in time, will turn back to ashes, back to cosmic dust to become another group of energy. Espiritu still exists. Then another creation happened in 1960, the year my present form was born.

I then realized that "Espiritu" is "Eternal". It was only my other physical body that died but it didn't end there, as it was transformed into another form of something. To think about it, we are living in a very huge cycle, a **"TIMELESS LIFETIME CYCLE"**.

In 1947, I was somebody,
Then I was nothing,
To become someone today.

BALANCE EXERCISES:

To balance the opposites, there should be a center. Try these few exercises to balance the opposites. Write your answers down.

* What will you do to balance the good from bad or vise versa?

Your Answer:

* What will you do to balance the positive from negative or vise versa?

Your Answer:

* What will you do to balance the known from unknown or vise versa?

Your Answer:

* What will you do to balance the young from old or vise versa?

Your Answer:

* What will you do to balance the east from west or vise versa?

Your Answer:

* What will you do to balance birth from death or vise versa?

Your Answer:

* What will you do to balance religion from science or vise versa?

Your Answer:

TOO MANY WORDS FOR AN ANSWER,
ARE THE DOORS TO CONFUSION;
SO LET

"NOTHING"

ANSWERS ALL THE QUESTIONS,
TO END THE SEPARATION.

* *

THE
BEGINNING

* *

OF MY STORY

THIS IS

THE
END

OF LIFE MYSTERIES

* *

THE SEARCH

* *

"Ask, and it will be given to you;
seek, and you will find;
knock, and it will be opened to you."
Matthew Chapter 7:7

"Come inside the house now, it is getting dark, and it is time for "**them**" to be out and play", Lolo (respect call for our grandfather) said.

"Who's them, Lolo?", I and my brothers asked.

"The unseen ones, the spirits of the dead", he said. "We have to respect them and give them a chance to be a part of this world, even though they are not seen anymore.

*"Oh, I see!", we said.

These few words I remembered what my grandfather had told when I was a child. They still fascinate me.

"To see the unseen?" Well, I think what we mean was we understood what he had said and obeyed what he told us.

Lolo was a very good man and I looked up to him as my very loving guardian. Before Lolo passed away, I had successive dreams that death was near him. He was the first one of my closest relatives who passed away. It really broke my heart when Lolo died as I thought I would never see him again. But I did see him again through my dreams and I felt his presence even though I was awake. He was still guarding me even though his physical body died.

29

* "Oh I see!" is not translated literally in the dialect we used.

When I felt his presence, I felt the comfort of love he gave me when he was still alive. Even though I didn't see Lolo's physical body anymore, he was still there with me, to comfort me when I needed him. Then I began to realized that death is nothing to be afraid of as death is only another part of life.

A month after my grandfather died, I thought of writing letters to the people who were seeking pen pals from the Philippines, my birth country. While I was writing a letter to one of the names from the newspaper, my inner voice told me to write the person who put in his ad "WILLING TO FALL IN LOVE". I followed what my inner voice told me which I normally do. I wrote a letter to the person in that ad. I didn't get any response from that person in the letter but he just showed-up without notice to my aunt's house where I stayed at that time. So, we met and talked about different things.

For the short time we met, I knew that, the man I just met would become my husband. We got married less than a month after we met. I was half the age of my husband but it didn't bother me as age didn't matter to me. He is a kind hearted man and a very generous person. As what one of my brothers said during our wedding, that even though one of our love ones passed on, another love one entered my life to fill that loss. The loss I felt when Lolo died.

My husband and I have different religion but we never talked about our religions. We both knew that if we talked about our religion, a family war starts. And we both don't want that to happen in our marriage, to fight over nothing. To argue religion is unnecessary.

To me, I couldn't ask any more than a husband like John. He provided me the things that I didn't have before, such as jewelries, a house, money, car, television, VCR, radio, computer, etc. He loves our family. We traveled different places and different countries and saw the things that I haven't seen before. I was full of all these things.

Then we started a business. To be a business-woman, a housewife, and a mother at the same time was a very stressfull and depressing job for me at that time.

I started to become a mean person. I didn't have any patience with other people especially with children who weren't behaving. I became a negative person. My mind was fixed on believing the things what I believed. I was tired all the time. I became a person that nobody wants to be around with, including myself. I became unhappy inside myself regardless of all the material possessions I had.

I started not loving myself. I became too fat for my height and was looking older faster than my normal age. My back already gave me trouble. My body already started to deteriorate. I started not taking care of myself. I was always depressed, especially when problems in the business came up.

My mind wasn't relaxed. My mind was always busy thinking how to make money to acquire more possessions.

I had lost my soul and I wanted it back to become a loving person again. I was searching for something I couldn't find. I stayed a negative person. I felt no peace inside me. I had felt my marriage was starting to fall apart.

Then, I started to pray solemnly to our Lord. I asked Him how could I go back to him without going to church every Sunday. I didn't want to go to church myself if my family was not with me. I couldn't force my husband to go with me to church to the religion in which I was baptized, as we are of different religions. Then suddenly, I heard an answer from within that gave me solace on my entire being. The reply was that I didn't need to go to church every Sunday just to go back to Him and that even though my husband and I have different religions but we both believe in one GOD, and **GOD** is **UNITY**. And if I will find my inner self back again to balance my outer self, then I will have a full life again.

The inner voice told me to teach what He had taught. I didn't have any idea what I'm going to teach as I didn't know what was taught. The only feelings I received was to LOVE MYSELF AGAIN, HAVE COMPASSION, HAVE PATIENCE AND UNDERSTANDING.

* *

FINDING THE GOLDEN KEY

* *

"For everyone who asks receives,
and he who seeks finds,
and to him who knocks it will be opened."

Matthew Chapter 7:8

Since then, I started to practice myself to keep silent when in time of confusion. I started practicing the sitting meditation and moving meditation such as Tai Chi Chuan and Hula Dance. I considered Hula Dance as my moving meditation, as when I danced, it keeps my mind relaxed.

Many months had passed and I was still busy with our business, with the housework, and with our two children. One day I was in my office, assorting mails, and trashing the "junk mails". Suddenly, my inner voice told me to pick up one of the "junk mail" which was to order a book titled "Ancient Secret of the Fountain of Youth" by Peter Kelder. By that time, I was not interested of studying about the Fountain of Youth. But my inner voice kept on telling me to pick that mail up and order the book. Again, I listened to my inner voice and ordered the book.

I read the book and the story fascinated me as it was very interesting. Which I recommend you to read. If you can't find that book to buy from the book stores or anywhere in your area, you can actually borrow the book from the public library.

Well, there were exercises in the book to follow and I started to practice the exercises. I encouraged my husband and my mother, who were always complaining about their body aches, to practice the exercises that were in the book. I also wanted to find out myself if the Fountain of Youth truly exists. My husband who is skeptical about the word reversing the aging process did some of the exercises with the other exercises he was doing, to loosen his back stiffness. My mother was very good in following the exercises which helped her arthritis.

I also kept on following the exercises that were in the book. The exercises helped me to encouraged myself to do other body movements. But for some reason, I felt there was still something missing.

I wondered to myself why when I practiced Tai Chi (Chinese meditation exercises) or if I danced Hula (Hawaiian dance), I felt my spirit moves with me during my body motions and why not the other exercises.

So, I started searching again.

One morning, during my sitting meditation I started to move my body so gently and did the movements that were in Peter Kelder's book. I was amazed what I felt, as if I was flying. My mind was relaxed and my body was relaxed. I felt my spirit was in motion and full.

"I found it!", I said to myself.

FOR EVERYONE WHO ASKS, RECEIVES "GOD"

GIFT OF DIVINITY

AND HE
WHO SEEKS,
FINDS

"LOVE

AND

PEACE"

LIFE

OMNIPOTENCE

VIRTUALITY

ETERNITY

PATIENCE

EDEN (PARADISE)

AWARENESS

CALMNESS

EASE

AND TO HIM
WHO KNOCKS,
IT WILL BE OPENED

"THE KNOWLEDGE OF UNDERSTANDING"

TO UNDERSTAND THE "SINGLE DIVINE PRINCIPLE" IS THE ONLY WAY TO THE FOUNTAIN OF YOUTH!

* *

JOURNEY GUIDE
TO
AWAKEN ESPIRITU

* *

To discover the profound treasure within
is to find the hidden door;
To open the hidden door,
is to have the golden key;
And the golden key can only be found,
to one who wants to believe the unseen.

As I mentioned before, our unseen world is the other half of our real world. The unseen is the world that most people have already forgotten how to live with. **It's so forgotten that most don't realize that we are actually living in the world that is invisible.** But it exist. Life can not exist without it.

ENERGY, CHI, KI, SPIRIT, PRANA, ESPIRITU, SOUL, FORCE, GHOST, WIND, AIR

These are few of the words we are using to define the unseen world. But do we really understand how they work? We like to study and work with them if we want to understand them. If we don't understand how they work, we are afraid of this invisible being and **fear causes to start the separation of the true meaning of the words above.**

THE HUMAN BODY

The human body has two kinds of body. One is the **physical (material) body** and the other, is the **spirit (energy) body**. These two are opposite from each other but one can not live without the other.

Our physical body is what we see in the mirror. We can see our eyes, nose, ears, mouth, hands, feet, etc. But do we really see our whole self?

Our physical body is just like a house. A house is not a home if no one lives in it. The physical body can not survive without it's spirit. If a spirit leaves ones body, is like a man walking out from his house to leave it empty and the house is no longer a home.

THE HUMAN MIND

Human has two minds. The **conscious** and the **subconscious**. These minds are opposite, but again, one cannot live without the other.

PHYSICAL BODY AND CONSCIOUS MIND

Almost all human beings are aware of these two, the physical and the conscious. These two **have been used consciously everyday** by human beings to keep one alive.

SPIRIT BODY AND SUBCONSCIOUS MIND

The spirit body and the subconscious mind are the other two that **are used everyday** to be alive **but were forgotten how to use them.**

THE SEPARATION OF THE OPPOSITES, WITHOUT CONSCIOUSLY AWARE OF IT, IS IMBALANCE.

We can see, smell, hear, taste and feel with our physical body but the physical body cannot do these things without the spirit.

The physical is material but not the spirit. **The spirit can only materialize itself to become physical.**

THE SEPARATION

To the person who puts all his attention to the material world is likely to forget the spirit world. And to the person who puts all his attention to the spirit world will then forget the material world.

These process will cause the separation of the single world into two.

MAKING THE TWO WORLDS INTO ONE

To balance these two worlds, we unite them back into one. To unite them back, we have to **open our awareness to what was separated.**

The separation of the whole world,
Will create their opposite sides:
North and South, East and West;
Equator is the only one in the center,
Where they meet to become even.

POSITIVE AND NEGATIVE

The **two forces** that one should **become aware of** are the **positive** and the **negative**.

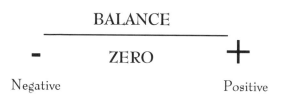

SCIENCE AND RELIGION ARE ONE

One should learn how to understand each word we are using everyday. Few word examples that science and religion are not totally different from each other, as their functions are the same:

SCIENTIFIC WORDS	RELIGIOUS WORDS
Energy / Force	Spirit / Ghost
Positive Energy	Good Spirit
Negative Energy	Evil Spirit
Recharge	Confess
Discharge	Exorcise
Good Condition	Sinless / Angel
Bad Condition	Sinful / Devil
Machine / Battery/ Human	Man

PHYSICAL AND METAPHYSICAL WORDS

The physical and metaphysical are not different from each other. They were separated by different words and were used differently that causes confusion to most people.

PHYSICAL WORDS	METAPHYSICAL WORDS
Telephone	Clairaudience
Television	Clairvoyance
Energy Field	Aura
Medical Healing	Faith Healing
Airplane	UFO
Physical Body	Spirit Body
Radio	Mental Telepathy
Exercise	Meditation
Birth or Death	Transformation
Energy	Chi / Ki / Prana
Antennas	ESP (Extra Sensory Perception)

To use a single word
is so simple to understand
than to use many words
that have never been understood.

UNDERSTANDING EACH WORD

Try to choose your own word in order for you to understand the meaning of it. When you understand the word you have choosen, pick up another word that is confusing to you and study it. **Start to become aware how each word works.** Study and practice each word you are interested in. Then study and practice each word that you are not interested in. **Remember to balance what you are studying and practicing.** Remember how to balance the opposites.

Too much attention on something,
has less learning
to communicate with nothing;
And to do much on nothing
cannot create something;
So to balance what you are working,
just be aware to go back to center,
to see both ends of what is happening.

We have to be aware of the two forces we are dealing in life, the positive and the negative.

A person who knows how a fully charged battery can make a machine work, should also understand how a man works if he is full in spirit.

For a person who knows how the process of a weak rechargeable battery has been charged, can also apply the same process to a weak human body.

FEW EXAMPLES OF THE WORD SEPARATIONS THAT CREATE THE "THIS IS RIGHT AND THAT IS WRONG" ATTITUDES ARE:

WORDS USED FOR MACHINE

When a non-rechargeable battery has already used up its energy, it will become useless. But when a rechargeable battery used up its energy, it can be recharged to become useful again.

As to recharge a dead battery, we put the positive side of the battery to the positive side of the charger. And the negative to negative. When the battery is fully charged, the battery can make a machine work again.

These words are accepted to most all of the human beings. As this is already scientifically proven.

WORDS USED FOR HUMAN

Think positive to become a positive person. A negative person always thinks negative.

These words are also been accepted to almost all mankind.

This process is the same way as to charge a re-chargeable battery. But the only difference is the positive and the negative were separated by two kinds of people.

APPLYING THE SCIENTIFICALLY PROVEN PROCESS OF A RECHARGEABLE BATTERY TO THE HUMAN BODY

The rechargeable battery is the closest physical thing that I can compare to our physical body. They have the same process on discharging, become weak or dead and revitalizing.

The battery uses energy in order to work, so are we. If we really study, practice, and understand how these things work, we can always renew ourselves whenever our energy is being used.

LAWS OF NATURE

The world is round, it begins from where it ends. It ends where it started. Our universe is infinite. God is invisible and perfect. God created us to dwell with and for us to be His children. God is everywhere. God created the Universe.

LAWS OF MAN

We are now living in the laws of man. To see it, is to believe it. Our mind has already been programmed to be born, grow old, and die for nobody is perfect. Our mind has been programmed to live the way man has followed it for centuries. Man has to pay his taxes when he is making something in order to follow the laws of man.

Man speeds up the process of the Laws of Nature. That creates destruction to our own self and to our own world.

Nothing is perfect,
And if we are not a thing,
We are perfect;
Nobody is perfect,
And if we have no body,
We are perfect;
Espiritu is not a thing;
Espiritu has no body,
Espiritu is perfect.

Espiritu is perfect until a man created its own laws to hasten the Laws of Nature.

KNOW THYSELF

To know oneself is important in one's life. Nobody can tell you who you really are. Even your own mother cannot tell you. If she does tell you and you don't understand, it will only cause the separation between both of you. **You are the only one who can find it out to understand it.**

ANCIENT PRACTICES AND TECHNIQUES

Meditation is one of the practices of the ancient to know thyself. Very few people have fully achieved this goal.

Meditation is a practice of being silent in both mind and body. It helps us to **remember** how **peaceful** it is to be silent.

RELAXING THE MIND AND BODY

Learn how to relax your mind. The body will follow when the mind is relaxed. The **spirit will move** when both mind and body are relaxed.

Relaxing the mind is similar to you relaxing the body muscles. Tension free, stress free, problem free, worry free, excitement free, thought free. **LET GO ALL** of the emotions, thoughts and feelings you have in order **to become free.**

A relaxed body is when you feel all the tensions of the body muscles, nerves and bones are relaxed. Let go all the tensions.

When your **mind** and **body** are **relaxed,** the **energy can circulate entirely** inside your whole self.

BEING CONSCIOUS ON THE UNCONSCIOUS

Start practicing to become aware of what is happening unconsciously in our daily routine in life. Such as breathing, sleeping, moving, drinking, eating, thinking, and other things we do unconsciously in order for us to survive. **Just remember the other half of what you are going to practice** which is also to be aware of what is happening consciously in our daily routine in life. Such as being a business person, being a parent, being an actor or actress, being a worker, etc. which we consciously know that we need to do it, in order for us and others to survive.

This way, we can keep ourselves in balance.

THE VITAL PROCESS

Proper breathing is our **vital process** in order for us **to awaken espiritu**.

If you observe a new born healthy baby breathing, you will notice that the baby breathes naturally down to their abdomen. As the baby grows to adulthood, their breathing becomes higher, up to their lungs. To those who are dying, they are just gasping for air in order to live. And to the dead, breathing is gone.

We started breathing since we enter inside our mother's womb. Still breathing until we decide to leave our body breathless.

PURE AIR AND POLLUTED AIR

Consider the pure air as positive and the polluted air as negative.

Human body's vital process is to **inhale pure air** and **exhale the polluted air.** Inhale the new and exhale the old.

If polluted air is inhaled, our whole body system will fill up with pollution. This causes the mind and body to function improperly.

PROGRAMMING

Everyday of our lives, we are programmed positively and negatively. We receive these programs from different sources such as watching TV and movies; listening to radio; hear people talking; reading books, newspapers or magazines; thoughts from other people; etc. We consciously and unconsciously receive all the positive and negative programs into ourselves. (See few examples of positive and negative programs on page 113)

LOVE AND HATE

Consider love as positive programming and hate as negative programming. These two opposites play an important part of our journey to awaken espiritu.

When practicing meditation, it is important to feel loved as to charge our mind and body with positive thoughts and feelings. Hatred is the negative feeling that needs to be discharged in order for the Laws of Nature to be followed.

TO LOVE THYSELF IS TO LOVE ALL!

JOURNEY TO YOUR WORLD WITHIN

Find yourself a comfortable place for you to practice meditation. It is better to do this practice with good ventilation. If you live in an area that has clean air, do your practice outside your house. If you live in an area that is polluted, it is better for you to do it inside your house. As long as your house has some house plants or has an air purifier with ozone, then it is safer to do your meditation. House plants or air purifier will help give breathable oxygen.

As mentioned before, we will charge our body with pure air (positive) and discharge the polluted air (negative). **This is important to be aware with this process as you will awake your Espiritu that could be good or bad, depending on the air you've inhaled.**

Early morning, between 4:00 a.m. to 9:00 a.m. is the best time to meditate especially when you do it with body motion. It is better to do this practice before you do anything else in the morning. By doing the ancient practice, this will help you prepare yourself how to deal with your daily life.

You can sit, stand, or lie down, whichever is comfortable for you to relax your mind and body. Make sure you are wearing comfortable clothes, so you'll have better energy circulation in your body.

After you have found your place for your meditation, put yourself in a comfortable position. Now, close your eyes or just focus your eyes on the tip of your nose.

Put the tip of your tongue on the roof of your mouth. If you are a male, put your left thumb on your navel and then put your right thumb on top of your left thumb. Vice versa for the ladies.

Before you start, tell yourself that nothing can disturb you on your journey within unless it's an emergency. And that you will come out slowly with a relaxed and calm mind after your journey within.

When you are ready, you exhale first and hold it for a few seconds. As to exhale the stale old air inside the body and inhale new fresh air. And then inhale through your nose down to your abdomen. Keep it natural. When you inhale, your abdomen should expand and not your chest. And when you exhale, the abdomen contracts. Some people find it easier for them to do this when they are laying down. Keep your mind relaxed. Focus your attention on your breathing until you are completely relaxed. Let all the tension go. Let your body relax and let all the tension in your body go.

When you feel a numbness in your body, just stay there for awhile. Let silence take over your world. It's so peaceful to be there in silence. Stay there for awhile.

When you are ready to go back out, slowly, let your mind go back to your breathing concentration. Then you can count from five to one and slowly open your eyes with your mind still relaxed and calmed.

Practice this first technique everyday. And when it is easier for you to do this first technique, you are ready for the next.

MEDITATION IN MOTION

The next ancient technique, is to meditate in motion. This is my favorite part, to move our relaxed body with a relaxed mind. As our espiritu will move too. This is the oneness of our whole being.

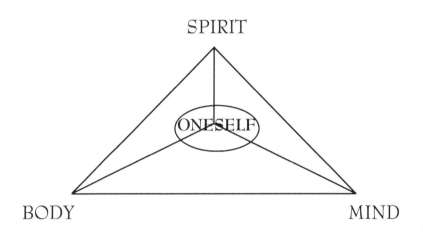

When the mind, body, and spirit
meet each other,
our divided self
will become one again.

This is the hardest part for a person to achieve. Constant and a lifetime practice is the only way to achieve it. Practice makes perfect.

When the three meet, it is worth it.

You can apply whatever movements you have learned from any books, instruction videos or from your instructors in your practice of meditation in motion. If you don't know any of the above, just use your daily movements, such as walking, turning your head from left to right, etc.

Hints for this technique:
1. Remember the vital process.
2. Keep the mind and body relaxed.
3. Aware of each movement separation such as paying attention on shifting the weight.
4. Remember to go back to center each time you do the opposite movements.
5. Move your body in slow motion in able for you to feel espiritu.
6. Be gentle with yourself.
7. Be patient.
8. Lifetime practice makes it perfect.

You will revitalize yourself if you will start practicing the motionless meditation or the moving meditation from 15 minutes to 1 hour a day.

Make a time for your own self to awaken your espiritu. 15 minutes to 1 hour in 24 hours is not much to ask to be with yourself, isn't it?

WHEN YOU BECOME A MASTER OF THIS ART, TIME IS NOTHING TO YOU AT ALL.

* *

LIVING IN HARMONY

* *

Learn to have *P*atience,

so your place is an *E*den,

to help open your *A*wareness,

to live in *C*almness

and *E*ase

These are the words what my Spirit Master told me. These words will always remind me to have patience with myself so I will have patience with everyone. I've noticed if I do something in a hurry or to rush somebody to do something, I speed up the functions of my nervous system. When my nervous system is not functioning properly, anger will start to rise. Anger is one of the negative feelings that causes a person to age. So to have patience, is helping me to keep myself calm and at ease so I will learn to **live in peace.**

BEING CENTERED

I've learned to live with both the seen and the unseen worlds. I've learned to balance the things that are not equal. I've learned to live with ancient and modern ways at the same time. This is the way of living that I'm going to teach to my children, and to those who sincerely want to learn, how to live in harmony.

CHALLENGES

Life is not exciting if there is no competition. That's why there are always opposites. We always encounter challenges everyday, whether we see it or not. Challenges always surround us and normally within our closest family and with our love ones. Challenge likes to play a tug of war game. This tug of war game makes a person angry, weak, jealous, hateful, tired, worried, and will become a negative person. The negative emotions that are felt causes a person to have a disease and to age.

LEARNING TO PLAY WITH CHALLENGE

I've noticed that when I used my own energy to play with challenge, it only caused my spirit to diminish. My energy will turn to waste. I then realized that to use my own force to play the tug of war game is not the way to play with challenge.

Yielding is how I've learned to play with this type of game. By yielding, I know nothing but winning.

WINNING BY YIELDING

If I become resentful, my body becomes rigid, which is a sign of old age. By not using any of my force to win is to gain me more spirit to vitalize myself. I've learned how to become flexible. When my mind is flexible, so is my body. This is how I win: by yielding.

UNBLOCKING THE NEGATIVE ENERGY

Consciously or unconsciously, our mind has been programmed with positive and negative energy all the time. We absorbed all kinds of energy in our mind. This creates the improper functions of the mind and body if the negative energy is trapped inside our systems.

Our physical body normally does its own job of processing and eliminating what we have eaten. In breathing, we inhale oxygen (O_2) and exhale carbon dioxide (CO_2) which normally happens in an area that is not polluted or has plenty of trees.

People inhale bad air and exhale bad air in polluted areas, where huge industries or active volcanoes create heavy smoke or where areas that people smoke tobacco. This is one of the reasons why there are many body and mind disorders in a crowded polluted areas. Thunderstorm can help cleanup the pollution in the air. Trees, plants, or an air purification equipment with ozone will also help an area to have a breathable air.

One has to decide for himself how and where to live in able to have a breathable air.

The mind absorbs all what one has seen, heard, tasted, smelt and felt. If one's mind is too busy thinking of doing something, the mind forgets to process and eliminate the negative thoughts and feelings that was absorbed. These negative thoughts and feelings that is still in the mind will become stagnant and makes the mind sick. If the mind is not at ease, so does the body. This is where the word disease comes from. When both mind and body are weak, the spirit starts to diminish and soon the spirit will leave one's body.

Learn to start paying attention to what your mind is absorbing. Pay attention on the positive and the negative programming. Let your mind rest for a little bit so it can also do its job of processing and eliminating what was absorbed. Start learning to take in the positive and take out the negative energy.

SLEEP TO DREAM

I haven't met anyone who does not sleep at all. **Sleeping is a natural process for the body to rest. It is a process of going to the spirit world**. This world is what we call **dream**. Even though we are sleeping, the mind is still working. The mind wonders around, that's why we dream. Dream is still a puzzle to most people. I interpret the meaning of my own dreams to guide and help me what to do in this physical world. Some people are gifted to interpret other peoples dream which I proudly say that one of them is my father, Amading. I encouraged my father to write a book about dream interpretations, which he did.

His book titled "Professor Swami Dream Interpretations plus Mole Significance". Fill out the order form to purchase his book.

LETTING THE MIND REST

Meditation is what I do in order for my mind to rest. I've learned to practice doing nothing to let the good flow of energy cleanse my mind and body. **Thinking is doing something and is a continuous job for the mind**. That's why I mentioned before that we forget the other half of one's life, which is the mind. Most people forget to let their mind rest. **We let our body rest by sleeping and we should let our mind rest by doing nothing**. Doing nothing is simply doing nothing at all.

BALANCED DIET

A balanced diet is also important for the body systems to function properly. I also recommend to drink at least eight glasses of purified drinking water a day.

PAST, PRESENT, AND FUTURE

Yesterday, I was born;
Today, I live;
Tomorrow, I will die.

I remember writing a poem with these three lines in it when I was in high school.

Today is the center of time. I found the center of all time by living in the present.

71

How I live my life in the present
is what my future will be.
What I've done today
will become my memories of yesterday.

* *

SEX UNITY

* *

With practice, it will become easier for a person to learn uniting oneself. One can start learning to unite it's opposite sex when oneself is already united.

Sex Unity is not done only through physical contact as what most people understood about the word sex.

Sex Unity can be done also through spirit contact. Even without using the physical body.

I will have more details regarding this subject in my future book.

A man and a woman,
are opposite from each other;
For them to become one,
they unite together.

* *

DANCING WITH SPIRIT

* *

I think of nothing,
but to dance with my spirit.

I love to dance with my spirit
and my spirit moves with me;
Yes, this is my little secret
to share with you
to find love and peace.

TAI CHI CHUAN

Tai means body and Chi is a Chinese word for vital energy. *Tai Chi Chuan* is a Chinese method of exercise where both the mind and body are relaxed. It is a meditation in motion. This is my magical dance and my masculine body motion.

I've learned the movements of the 37 Yang Short Form of Tai Chi Chuan from a video tape I purchased. The instructor of the tape was Terry Dunn. I considered him as my good teacher on tape. I devotedly followed his instructions that was on the tape. At first, my whole body was aching as my mind wasn't relaxed enough to follow instructions. It took me six months to memorize all the movements. After I've memorized the whole form, I began to practice it constantly every morning.

There are many forms and names of Tai Chi Chuan. Forms that were created from different Tai Chi Masters.

I started to understand Tai Chi Chuan when my spirit started to move with me during the practice. When my spirit moves with me, I created another form of Tai Chi Chuan.

HULA DANCE

"I'm going to be a Hula dancer someday", I said to myself when I first saw a Hula dancer dance during my high school days in the Philippines. The dream I had to become a Hula dancer became a reality to me.

Hula Dance is an ancient Hawaiian dance. Hula is not just an ordinary dance. Understanding the profound meaning of Hula is understanding and knowing thyself. This is the reason why I love this beautiful ancient dance.

I am grateful to have talented Hula teachers who taught me different movements of the dance. My Hula teachers are always part of me especially when I dance.

Whoever watches a real Hula dancer dance can also feel the feelings of the dancer. The feelings of love, loneliness, togetherness, depending on the emotions that is felt inside by the dancer. A real Hula dancer can give out a magic of love that can touch everyones heart.

Hula dance is my masculine and feminine body motions.

ALSHARQI DANCE
(pronounced ^ash-sh^ar-qe)

I've learned this beautiful body movements from my good friend, Karen, who loves this ancient Oriental Dance.

Each body movements has its own mystery. Each motion practices the separation of the opposites and then going back to center.

This is my feminine body motion.

Tai Chi is the thing I do
To Hula the stress away
So Alsharqi will keep me company.

* *

CONSTANT CHANGE

* *

Our lives are constantly changing. I found out myself that it is easier to follow the flow of energy to where it's going. This is what I call **destiny**. Destiny to me is the answer to my prayers. To resist the flow of energy only causes the delay of my destination.

PRAYERS

We ask something when we pray. Our mind talks and talks, asking for the things we need.

I have to let my mind stop talking in order for me to hear the answers of my prayers.

I'VE LEARNED TO LISTEN

My mind can only hear the answers of my prayers when my mind stops thinking and talking. This is how I listen to my spirit guide. This process of listening is the same way as we stop talking with our mouth in order for us to hear what the other person is saying.

MOVING FROM PLACE TO PLACE

My family and I moved from one place to another. Each place we moved to had different energy. Every place we've lived affects our lifestyle depending on what kind of energy that is on the area.

On May 1995, on my way back home to New Mexico from the Philippines where I held a seminar, I stopped by to see Molokai, Hawaii. My husband had told me to visit at Molokai. He had told me to follow my own feelings about the area, which I did.

To make the story short, we moved to Molokai, Hawaii in July 1995. There are no movie houses, no malls, no big department stores and no university on the island. Some people asked us why we moved to this island. I only respond to them that there was some kind of energy that pulled us to this area. I didn't really know at that time the real reason why until I started to understand what is "Nothing".

* *

I KNOW "NOTHING" BETTER

* *

Few months since we moved to Molokai, my husband and our teenage son, Ryan, started to get bored. They claimed that they missed something as they see nothing on the island. They are afraid that nothing will ever happen to our lives that are exciting. My husband who is not used of an island climate decided that we should move again. Our son seconded the motion. This is a tug of war game for us as our daughter and I don't really want to move so soon.

Few days after we talked about moving, I felt my back shoulder was aching. It was hurting for about a week. I couldn't turned my head to the side as it was really hurting. I wondered why it started aching and what had caused it. I then realized that I became resentful of having to move again. As soon as I found out what had caused it, I then unblocked the negative energy which was resentment. I started to yield and accepted my husband's wish to move to a place where he wants to live. After I unblocked the negative energy, my back shoulder stopped aching.

Yes, I see nothing in Molokai, Hawaii but this is not what all I saw. This is the place where I've learned to understand "NOTHING". I know "NOTHING" better when I started to understand this profound knowledge.

Wherever I go, wherever I will be, I will always have "NOTHING" with me. This way, I will always create something.

* *

MAGICAL THOUGHTS

* *

Farewell to the idea of being weak,

Or being old as you can see,

Rejuvenate ourselves is what we do and say,

Eager to reveal these profound secrets that

Very few ever understood how to be young eternally;

Excited are we to first learn this mystery by

Relaxing our mind to vitalize our body.

Yes, "The Fountain of Youth" truly exists,

Only to those who firmly believe,

Use the ancient practices and techniques;

Nurture the spirit with love and faith,

Glory to those who have fully achieved!

Children who like to surround us,

love to train us to keep our energy;

Until it is time for them to become aware that

believing is our magic to victory.

* *

FOREVER YOUNG Club®

* *

In April 1993, my inner voice told me to start a club and call it "FOREVER YOUNG CLUB" which I started on May 1993.

Forever Young Club is a division of Air & Water King, Inc., a Nevada Corporation, and was registered on February 21, 1994 in the State of New Mexico with the logo of "FOREVER YOUNG Club". Considering the Air & Water King is our physical business, thus Forever Young Club is spiritual. This is how I balance my everyday life by doing the physical and spiritual at the same time.

The Club is growing internationally. Rejuvenation classes, special and annual events, seminars and workshops are the activities of the Club. There is no age limit to become a member (parent's/guardian's permission to minors). To qualify, one should be a non-smoker, non-alcoholic, non-drug addicted, or willing to quit these vices. Members will receive quarterly newsletters and have the opportunity to share their amazing experiences with others. Valuable discounts on products, classes and workshops are given to club members.

Annual membership fee is only US$24.00 in U.S.A. and in the Philippines. Other countries are US$32.00 annual fee. **To those who reach 100 years of age, membership is FREE**.

Fill up the Forever Young Club membership application form if you are interested of joining the club. Members will receive International Membership card.

The Forever Young Club is proud to say that on the date this book was written, we have our first member who is 100 years young. Her name is Gladys Iris Clark, who is an author of a book titled "FOREVER YOUNG". Her story is also fascinating and interesting. You can purchase her book directly from her at 205 Sunset Drive, Box 110, Sedona, Arizona 86336 U.S.A.

* *

NOTE FROM THE AUTHOR

* *

Some of the words from this book came from my Spirit Master who revealed these profound secrets to me and wanted me to share them to those who are seeking.

I recommend for you to read this book more than once so it will be understood freely.

Use your God given gift wisely when you come to realize it. Unused or misuse will only create destruction to oneself.

This book is purposely not copyrighted as this is an open book to everyone. I captured the thoughts from the universe and materialized them in writing. These magical thoughts are all ours to share. I let the "Knowledge of Understanding" flow freely in order for us to be free from greed.

No part of this book will be sealed in order for us to follow the Laws of Nature.

In able for our whole world to be peaceful, one should start learning to find that peace within. If one finds it, then there will be peace in their home, in their community, in their country, and in the whole world.

Let us begin to live in peace so we don't have to wait to rest in peace.

This book is protected under the Laws of Nature.

ACKNOWLEDGEMENT

I would like to thank my Spirit Master who helped and guided me the things that needs to be written to materialized the invisible. I thank to all who helped made my thoughts become a book so it will be visible for others to read and benefit from it. My gratitude to my love ones who are also part of my story.

ABOUT THE AUTHOR

Angelie Bliss, Ms.D. (Doctor of Metaphysics) is the President and Founder of the Forever Young Club. She is also the Secretary/Treasurer of Air & Water King, Inc. She is still involved working on their business in Truth or Consequences, New Mexico. Even though she is not physically present at their business in New Mexico, she uses the known mysteries to do her part on the business. She is trilingual. She manages herself as a business woman, a poet, an artist, a traveler, accountant, book-keeper, computer operator, Hula dancer, Alsharqi dancer, Tai Chi and Yoga practitioner, a housewife and mother of two children. She holds classes and workshops in different places. She teaches Tai Chi for Longevity with Polynesian and Alsharqi Techniques. She loves to perform Hula, Alsharqi and Tai Chi dance to the public.

She is presently creating another art of her life, a book author.

Her motto:
"I BELIEVE THAT EVERYTHING IS POSSIBLE!"

To get in touch with her, write to Forever Young Club, 520 Broadway, New Mexico 87901 U.S.A.

Angelie Bliss
picture taken January 18, 1995
during the Forever Young Club's 1st annual event
"Trip to the Land of Paradise"

NEXT BOOK TITLES

I   Tai Chi for Longevity
with Polynesian and Alsharqi Techniques
Publication date 1997

II   Learn and Understand the Magic of Sex Unity
Publication date 1998

III   Spirit of Aloha Mystery
Publication date ?

BOOKS FOR YOUR THOUGHTS

AGELESS BODY - TIMELESS MIND
by Deepak Chopra, M.D.

ANCIENT SECRET OF THE
FOUNTAIN OF YOUTH
by Peter Kelder

FOREVER YOUNG
by Earlyne Chaney, Ph.D.

FOREVER YOUNG
A MANUAL FOR REJUVENATION
AND LONGEVITY
by Gladys Iris Clark

FOREVER YOUNG
20 YEARS YOUNGER IN 20 WEEKS
by Stuart M. Berger, M.D.

PROFESSOR SWAMI
DREAM INTERPRETATIONS
plus MOLE SIGNIFICANCE
by Amading Abad

GLOSSARY

AKUA - Hawaiian word for God

ALSHARQI - half-English and half-Arabic phrase referring to the refined Oriental dances of the Middle East.

AURA - Energy field

CLAIRAUDIENCE - the power of hearing something not present to the ear but regarded as having objective reality

CLAIRVOYANCE - the power or ability to perceive matters beyond the range of ordinary perception

CONFUCIUS - an ancient Chinese philosopher

DIVOS - Philippine word for God

FENG SHUI - an ancient Chinese science that gives someone good suggestions on finding an ideal place to live.

LAO TZU - a Chinese philosopher who founded Taoism in the 6th century B.C.

METAPHYSICS - beyond the physical

OMNIPOTENCE - force of unlimited power

REIKI - an ancient Japanese method of spiritually guide healing

QABALA - an ancient word of the earliest form of Jewish mysticism

REINCARNATION - a rebirth of a soul in a new human body

SHAMAN - one who uses magic for the purpose of curing the sick, divining the hidden, and controlling events

TAO - the creative principle that orders the universe as conceived by Taoists

TELEKINESIS - mind over matter

VIRTUALITY - essence; ultimate nature of a thing especially as opposed to its existence

VOODOO - South African / South American word used for their ancient mysticism

YOGA - a Hindu activity of body, mind, and spirit

PROGRAM EXAMPLES

POSITIVE	NEGATIVE
LOVE	HATE
COURAGE	FEAR
PEACE	WAR
HAPPY	SAD
EASE	DISEASE
PATIENCE	IMPATIENCE
TRUST	SUSPICIOUS
CALM	NERVOUS
CAN	CANNOT
FAITH	DISBELIEF
COMPASSION	JEALOUSY
YOUNG	OLD
FLEXIBLE	RIGID
HEALTHY	SICKLY
RELAXED	TENSE
POSSIBLE	IMPOSSIBLE
SUCCESS	FAILURE
LAUGHTER	CRY
ALIVE	DEAD
BLISSFUL	WORRIED

FOREVER YOUNG Club®
MEMBERSHIP APPLICATION

Date: _____

Name: _____

(Please Print)   First   Middle   Last

Physical Address: _____

_____

Mailing Address: _____

_____

Telephone: _____

Date of Birth: _____

             Month   Day   Year

Age: _____

Signature of Applicant: _____

Please return this application form with your fees to:

FOREVER YOUNG Club®
520 Broadway
Truth or Consequences
New Mexico 87901 U.S.A.

Please check one:
[ ] US$ 24.00 - U.S.A. & Philippines Annual membership fees
[ ] US$ 32.00 - Other countries Annual membership fees

NOTE: To those who are 100 years of age and over, please send only this application with proof of age.

FOREVER YOUNG Club®
MEMBERSHIP APPLICATION

Date: _____

Name: _____

(Please Print)   First   Middle   Last

Physical Address: _____

_____

Mailing Address: _____

_____

Telephone: _____

Date of Birth: _____

               Month   Day   Year

Age: _____

Signature of Applicant: _____

Please return this application form with your fees to:

FOREVER YOUNG Club®
520 Broadway
Truth or Consequences
New Mexico 87901 U.S.A.

Please check one:
[ ] US$ 24.00 - U.S.A. & Philippines Annual membership fees
[ ] US$ 32.00 - Other countries Annual membership fees

NOTE: To those who are 100 years of age and over, please send only this application with proof of age.

ORDER FORM

Air & Water King, Inc.

520 Broadway, Truth or Consequences
New Mexico 87901 U.S.A.
(505) 894-2441

FYC Member#_____ (Must be provided to receive discount)

Name_____

Address_____

City_____ State_____ Zip_____

Country_____ Phone#_____

Quantity	Book Title	Unit Cost	Total Cost
_____	I discovered the Ancient Secrets of the Fountain of Youth! - "The Golden Key to Unlock the Hidden Door of the Profound Treasure Within"	US$ 12.95	US$_____
_____	Professor Swami Dream Interpretations plus Mole Significance	US$ 12.95	US$_____
		Subtotal	US$_____

For total order less than $100.00 deduct 10%discount (_____)
For total order $100.00 and above deduct 15% discount (_____)

Discounts apply only to Forever Young Club Members

New Mexico residents, add 6.5625% tax   US$_____

Shipping and Handling   US$_____

TOTAL AMOUNT DUE   US$_____

THANK YOU FOR YOUR ORDER

TO ALL DISTRIBUTORS, PLEASE CALL OR WRITE FOR DISTRIBUTOR PRICES

[ ] Check or Money Order
Charge to: [ ] Visa [ ] Mastercard [ ] Discover
Credit Card Number_____
Expiration Date_____
Signature as it appears on credit card_____

SHIPPING & HANDLING for U.S.A.

For Orders totaling	Include	For Orders totaling	Include
Up to $ 25.00	$ 4.50	$ 50.01 - $ 75.00	$ 7.50
$ 25.01 - $ 50.00	$ 5.50	$ 75.01 - $100.00	$ 8.50
		Over $ 100.00	$10.00

International Orders: Please submit international Money Order or bank draft payable in U.S. funds.
Shipping & Handling for Canada - Add $ 3.50 to the domestic rates.
For International - Add $ 7.50 to the domestic rates. For orders over $ 175.00 add 10% of the order to domestic rates. International orders sent by surface rate may take 2 to 3 months.

ORDER FORM

Air & Water King, Inc.

520 Broadway, Truth or Consequences
New Mexico 87901 U.S.A.
(505) 894-2441

FYC Member#_____ (Must be provided to receive discount)

Name_____

Address_____

City_____ State_____ Zip_____

Country_____ Phone#_____

Quantity	Book Title	Unit Cost	Total Cost
_____	I discovered the Ancient Secrets of the Fountain of Youth! - "The Golden Key to Unlock the Hidden Door of the Profound Treasure Within" US$ 12.95		US$_____
_____	Professor Swami Dream Interpretations plus Mole Significance US$ 12.95		US$_____

Subtotal   US$_____

For total order less than $100.00 deduct 10%discount   (_____)
For total order $100.00 and above deduct 15% discount (_____)
Discounts apply only to Forever Young Club Members

New Mexico residents, add 6.5625% tax   US$_____
Shipping and Handling   US$_____
TOTAL AMOUNT DUE   US$_____

THANK YOU FOR YOUR ORDER

TO ALL DISTRIBUTORS, PLEASE CALL OR WRITE FOR DISTRIBUTOR PRICES

[ ]Check or Money Order
Charge to: [ ]Visa [ ]Mastercard [ ]Discover
Credit Card Number_____
Expiration Date_____
Signature as it appears on credit card_____

SHIPPING & HANDLING for U.S.A.

For Orders totaling	Include	For Orders totaling	Include
Up to $ 25.00	$ 4.50	$ 50.01 - $ 75.00	$ 7.50
$ 25.01 - $ 50.00	$ 5.50	$ 75.01 - $100.00	$ 8.50
		Over $ 100.00	$10.00

International Orders: Please submit international Money Order or bank draft payable in U.S. funds.
Shipping & Handling for Canada - Add $ 3.50 to the domestic rates.
For International - Add $ 7.50 to the domestic rates. For orders over $ 175.00 add 10% of the order to domestic rates. International orders sent by surface rate may take 2 to 3 months.

ORDER FORM

Air & Water King, Inc.
520 Broadway, Truth or Consequences
New Mexico 87901 U.S.A.
(505) 894-2441

FYC Member#_____ (**Must be provided to receive discount**)
Name_____
Address_____
City_____ State_____ Zip_____
Country_____ Phone#_____

Quantity	Book Title	Unit Cost	Total Cost
_____	I discovered the Ancient Secrets of the Fountain of Youth! - "The Golden Key to Unlock the Hidden Door of the Profound Treasure Within"	US$ 12.95	US$_____
_____	Professor Swami Dream Interpretations plus Mole Significance	US$ 12.95	US$_____

Subtotal US$_____
For total order less than $100.00 deduct 10%discount (_____)
For total order $100.00 and above deduct 15% discount (_____)
Discounts apply only to Forever Young Club Members

New Mexico residents, add 6.5625% tax   US$_____
Shipping and Handling   US$_____
TOTAL AMOUNT DUE   US$_____

THANK YOU FOR YOUR ORDER

TO ALL DISTRIBUTORS, PLEASE CALL OR WRITE FOR DISTRIBUTOR PRICES

[ ]Check or Money Order
Charge to: [ ]Visa [ ]Mastercard [ ]Discover
Credit Card Number_____
Expiration Date_____
Signature as it appears on credit card_____

SHIPPING & HANDLING for U.S.A.

For Orders totaling	Include	For Orders totaling	Include
Up to $ 25.00	$ 4.50	$ 50.01 - $ 75.00	$ 7.50
$ 25.01 - $ 50.00	$ 5.50	$ 75.01 - $100.00	$ 8.50
		Over $ 100.00	$10.00

International Orders: Please submit international Money Order or bank draft payable in U.S. funds.
Shipping & Handling for Canada - Add $ 3.50 to the domestic rates.
For International - Add $ 7.50 to the domestic rates. For orders over $ 175.00 add 10% of the order to domestic rates. International orders sent by surface rate may take 2 to 3 months.